Awesome Air

by Rena Korb

illustrations by Brandon Reibeling

Content Consultant:

Julian Marshall, Ph.D. • Professor of Environmental Engineering • University of Minnesota

visit us at www.abdopublishing.com

Published by Magic Wagon, a division of the ABDO Publishing Group, 8000 West 78th Street, Edina, Minnesota, 55439. Copyright © 2008 by Abdo Consulting Group, Inc. International copyrights reserved in all countries. All rights reserved. No part of this book may be reproduced in any form without written permission from the publisher. Looking Glass Library™ is a trademark and logo of Magic Wagon.

Printed in the United States.

Text by Rena Korb
Illustrations by Brandon Reibeling
Edited by Nadia Higgins
Interior layout and design by Ryan Haugen
Cover design by Brandon Reibeling

Library of Congress Cataloging-in-Publication Data

Korb, Rena B.
  Awesome air / Rena Korb ; illustrated by Brandon Reibeling ; content consultant, Julian Marshall, Ph.D.
    p. cm. — (Science rocks!)
  ISBN 978-1-60270-036-9
  1. Air—Juvenile literature. I. Reibeling, Brandon, ill. II. Title.
  QC161.2.K67 2008
  551.5—dc22
                        2007006320

Table of Contents

Amazing Air

What is something you can't see but is all around you? What makes the wind whisper through the trees? What holds an airplane in the sky?

The answer to all these questions is air.

What Is Air?

Hold out your hands and run as fast as you can. Air brushes against your fingertips.

You can't see air, but you know it's there. You can feel it. Air is a mixture of invisible gases.

Air's Power

Air has weight. Your bedroom could have 100 pounds (45 kilograms) of air in it!

Then why aren't you squashed?
You can't feel air's weight because
it is pushing at you from all directions.

When air moves, it creates wind.

Wind pushes clouds across the sky.
It makes flags flutter and papers
fly from your backpack.

Strong tornado winds can turn over a car,
lift the roof off a house, or even carry away a cow.

Air for Life

Put your hands on your chest, and take a deep breath. What happens? Your chest rises because your lungs are filling with air.

Oxygen from air flows into your body.

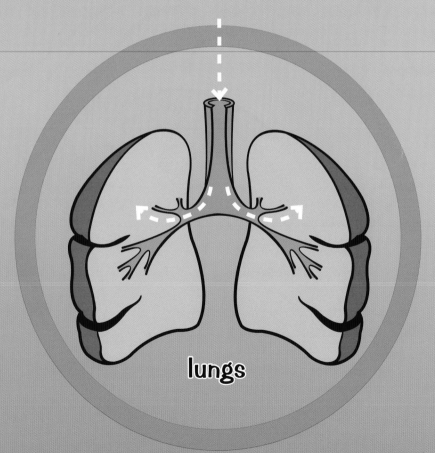

lungs

You could live only a few minutes without oxygen.

All plants and animals need oxygen, too.

Fish also breathe oxygen, but they don't get it from the air. Instead, they use their gills to get oxygen from the water.

Air and Sound

Imagine you're saying your name.
Your lips move, but no sound comes out.
That is how it would be without air.

Sound travels through air like waves traveling
through water. It carries the noises of your
world around you.

Useful Air

Has your bike ever had a flat tire? What happened?

Air leaked out of the tire. The tires on your bike need air to keep them rolling. So do tires on cars, trucks, and buses.

Air fills the little pockets in bubble wrap, too. The air acts like a cushion. It keeps things from breaking in the mail.

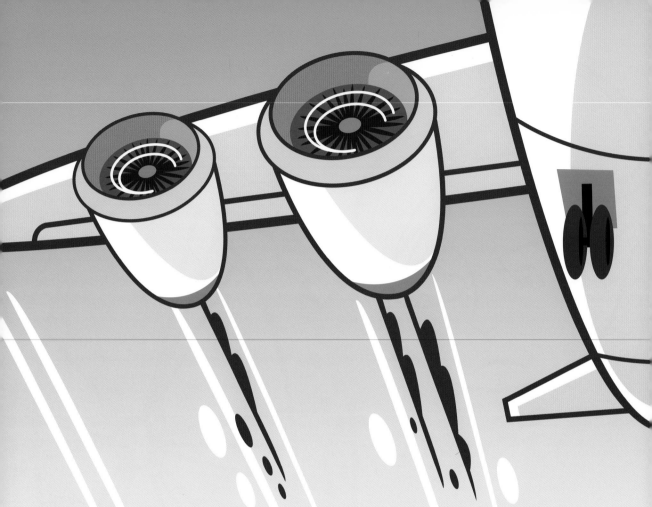

Air fills the sails on sailboats and pushes them along the water. Air gets under the wings of birds and flies them through the sky.

Air is even strong enough to hold up an airplane!

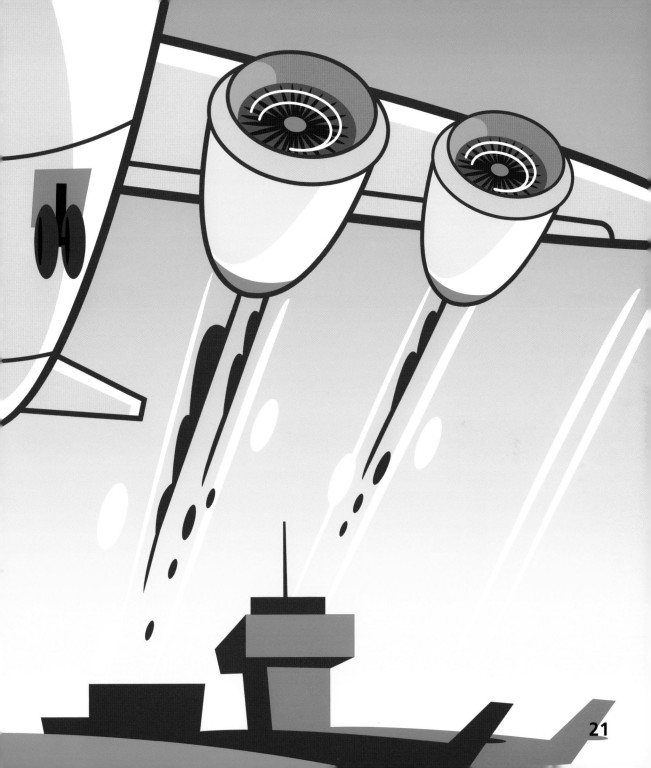

The Atmosphere

Like a blanket, air surrounds our planet.
This layer of air surrounding Earth is called
the atmosphere.

The atmosphere protects all living things.

The atmosphere goes up about 22 miles
(35 kilometers) into the sky. There is less air this high up.
Finally, the atmosphere disappears into space.

The atmosphere blocks out many
of the sun's harmful rays.
But it lets helpful rays pass
through to Earth.

The atmosphere traps
the heat from the sun.
It makes our world
warm enough for life to grow.

Keeping Air Clean

Everything on Earth needs air.
But smoke from cars and
factories can make air dirty.
Air pollution can make people sick.
It can kill plants and animals.

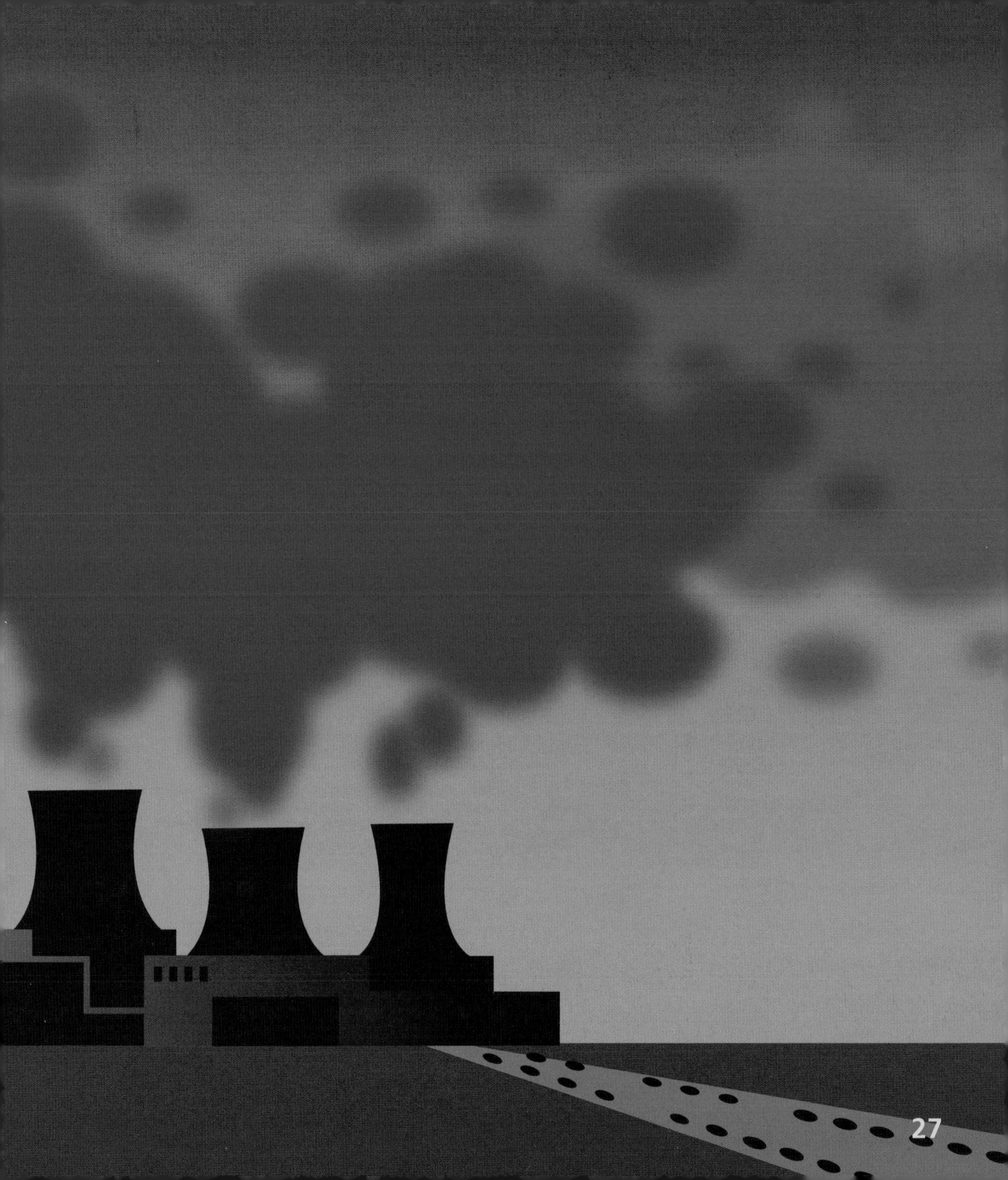

You can help keep air clean.
Walk instead of drive. Saving electricity
helps, too. So remember to turn off the lights.

It's everyone's job to protect the air.
After all, even though we can't see air,
it keeps us alive!

Activity

See the Power of Air

What you need:

A balloon

Several heavy books

What to do:

1. Put the balloon on the edge of a ledge or a table. Make sure you will be able to blow the balloon up where you have placed it.

2. Pile the books on top of the balloon. Make sure the body of the balloon is under the books and the lip of the balloon is free so you can blow it up.

3. Blow up the balloon. As you do, air will be making it bigger. What happens to the books? Are you surprised by the power of air?

Fun Facts

People breathe in oxygen and breathe out carbon dioxide. Plants do just the opposite. They breathe in carbon dioxide and breathe out oxygen. In this way, people and plants help each other.

When Earth first formed, there was little oxygen in the air. As years passed, plants breathed out more and more oxygen. After a few billion years, there was enough oxygen in the air for people and animals to live.

There is less air high on a mountain than at its bottom. As people climb up a mountain, they find it harder to breathe. However, people who live in high places have no trouble breathing. Their bodies have gotten used to getting less air.

Divers in the ocean carry tanks filled with air for breathing. These scuba tanks let them explore deep under the water.

Orville and Wilbur Wright invented the first airplane. They studied birds to learn how to build the wings of their plane.

Glossary

atmosphere—the layer of air surrounding Earth.

gases—substances that spread out to fill up any container they are in, like air in a tire; gases do not keep their own shape like a solid or level off inside a cup like a liquid.

lungs—a pair of body parts in the chest that fill up with air and send oxygen into the blood.

oxygen—a gas in the air that people breathe into their lungs; oxygen helps keep people alive.

pollution—harmful substances that dirty the air.

On the Web

To learn more about air, visit ABDO Publishing Company on the World Wide Web at **www.abdopublishing.com**. Web sites about air are featured on our Book Links page. These links are routinely monitored and updated to provide the most current information available.

Index

32